THE MYTH

OF

OVER-POPULATION

By
ROUSAS J. RUSHDOONY

THE CRAIG PRESS
Nutley, New Jersey
1971

UNIVERSITY SERIES: Historical Studies

Rousas J. Rushdoony, Editor

Library of Congress Catalogue Card No. 73-81505

Printed in the United States of America

TABLE OF CONTENTS

WHAT IS OVER-POPULATION?

Increasingly, modern man has come to believe that he faces a serious problem in the near future because of the so-called population explosion. The world, he is told, is running out of room and out of food for man, and, as a result, drastic measures may be necessary in order to prevent disaster.

Before the question, "Does the world face over-population?" can be answered, another question must be faced: "What is over-population?"

Perhaps the best answer to this latter question is that over-population is an imbalance between the number of people living and their food supply, which results in hunger and even famine because the available production of food cannot match the population's needs.

In terms of this definition, it must be recognized that the world has had the problem of over-population several hundred times at least, and probably almost consistently during much of its history. This ancient problem of over-population can best be understood by a few illustrations, and first of all, its history in North America. North America had a continuing problem of over-population before the coming of the white man. The Indian population was small, perhaps at most 250,000 to 300,000, and perhaps even less than half that number. Nevertheless, over-population was a continual problem, and it led to hunger, famine, and cannibalism. The very word "cannibal" comes from the Americas. It is derived from the Spanish *Canibales*, which came from the Carib *calina, galibi*, literally, strong men, i.e., those who practiced it. Both among the tribes contacted by Columbus and in the areas now a part of the United States, cannibalism was fairly prevalent. Its purpose was certainly often religious and magical, but it was also clearly economical as well, often dictated by the shortage of food. Among some tribes, its magical use continued into the 19th century:

> From time immemorial the Skidi Pawnees had offered a human sacrifice to the morning star each spring in order to insure the success of their crops of corn, beans, and pumpkins. The victim was always a prisoner of war, and usually a pure young woman. She was treated kindly by her captors and kept in ignorance of her fate until the morning she was led, painted from head to foot in sacred red and black colors, to a scaffold in the center of the village, tied to the crossbars, and, just as the morning star appeared in the sky, killed by a medicine arrow shot through her heart.[1]

This is clearly a case of human sacrifice; human sacrifice was often accompanied by a ritual act of cannibalism. But there also existed extensive cannibalism as a remedy for hunger. Indian cannibalism is very little reported or studied. Older Indians who recalled it were unwilling to discuss readily a subject which brought much disrepute to them. Modern writers, prone to a romantic view of the Indians, tend to mention it only in passing and then to justify it by unfavorable references to cruelty in Western civilization.[2] Most general works give us only a brief, passing reference to such facts as this, concerning a South American people: "some of the many bands of Tupian people bred their women to captives of war and raised the resultant children like veal calves for butchering."[3] In most cases, however, cannibalism for economic reasons was a last resort, although not an uncommon last resort.

Why were the Indians hungry, when they had the wealth of the Americas at their disposal? The answer is that their food supply was severely limited. A few animals, like the passenger pigeon, were seasonally plentiful, but they were not always available. Before the white man brought the horse and the gun to the Indians, buffalo

[1] John C. Ewers: *Artists of the Old West*, p. 48. New York: Doubleday & Co., 1965.
[2] Oliver La Farge: *A Pictorial History of the American Indian*, p. 56. New York: Crown Publishers, 1957.
[3] William Brandon, with Alvin M. Josephy, Jr.: *The American Heritage Book of Indians*, p. 56. American Heritage Publishing Co., 1961.

were much more difficult to hunt, and smaller game was normally depended on. In forested areas, game was scarce. Living off the land is a poor way to live and makes only a marginal and precarious existence possible. It was rarely done by white men. The fur trappers went into the wilderness with food and equipment as their capital: a grubstake made survival possible. Settlers moved out in large groups, with at least two years' income as capital, to clear, plant, and develop the soil. As the settlers developed the soil, the nearby game increased, because the food supply increased. Game drew close to settlements and multiplied and Indians drew close to settlers to get the game as well as the settlers' produce and animals. The coming of the white man increased the food supply, because the white man developed the earth.[4]

Here is the key to the problem. The total Indian population in North America was not greater than many an average-sized American city, and yet the Indians were unable to produce enough food to avoid famine. Some counties in California today produce more food than perhaps the Indians of North, South, and Central America ever saw in a year. For hunting tribes, famine was a normal thing.

> From the Abnaki of Maine through the Micmac of Nova Scotia and the Montagnais and Naskapi of Quebec and Labrador, hunger was increasingly a part of life and legend, in direct proportion as farming dwindled and hunting became the only gainful occupation. Even in a country teeming, as the saying goes, with game, the chase is bound to be a shaky provider, there being nothing stable about a supply of wild meat.[5]

Agriculture then was a preventative to famine, but it was not a certain preventative. Repeatedly, the farming peoples of Europe have undergone famine. Thus, in England alone, during the 13th century, hunger and famine struck in 1203, 1209, 1224, 1235, 1239, 1243, 1257, 1258, 1271, 1286, 1289, 1294, 1295, and 1298. In 1258,

[4] See James C. Malin:.The Grassland of North America: Prolomena to Its History, pp. 138-140, Lawrence, Kansas; 1947; and Malin, "The Grassland of North America: its Occupancy and the Challenge of Continuous Reappraisals," p. 10, Background Paper No. 19, prepared for the Wenner-Gren Foundation International Symposium, "Man's Role in Changing the Face of the Earth," Princeton Inn, Princeton, New Jersey, June 16-22, 1955. See also Marquis de Chastellex: Travels in North America in the Years 1780, 1781, and 1782, vol. I, p. 79f., Chapel Hill: University of North Carolina Press, 1963.

[5] Brandon, op. cit., p. 175.

for example, it was reported that the poor ate the bark of trees, and horseflesh, and that 20,000 starved in London, which was the report also for 1235. In 1239, we are told that people ate their children, and 1286, a 23 years' famine began, with the years cited above being simply the severest years.[6]

The Plymouth colony in New England faced famine immediately as a result of its farming. The cause for this is stated candidly by Bradford: it was the socialistic system of farming which created the famine:

> At length, after much debate of things, the Govr (with the advice of the cheefest among them) gave way that they should set corne every man for his owne particuler, and in that regard trust to them selves; in all other things to goe on in the generall way as before. And so assigned to every family a parcell of land, according to the proportion of their number for that end, only for present use (but made no devission for inheritance), and ranged all boys and youths under some famillie. This had very good success; for it made all hands very industrious, so as much more corne was planted then other waise would have bene by any means the Govr or any other could use, and saved him a great deall of trouble, and gave farr better contente. The women now wente willingly into the feild, and tooke their little-ones with them to set corne, which before would aledg weaknes, and inabilitie; whom to have compelled would have bene thought great tiranie and oppression.

> The experience that was had in this commone course and condition, tried sundrie years, and that amongst godly and sober men, may well evince the vanitie of that conceite of Platos and other ancients, applauded by some of later times;—that the taking away of propertie and bringing in communitie into a comone wealth, would make them happy and florishing; as if they were wiser than God. For this communitie (so farr as it was) was found to breed much confusion and discontent, and retard much imployment that would have been to their benefite and comforte.[7]

The problem at Plymouth Plantation was thus a restrictive form of farming, one imposed from London, which undercut initiative and production. Basic to sound farming, therefore, is freedom from

[6] E. Parmalee Prentice: *Hunger and History, The Influence of Hunger on Human History*, p. 6f. Caldwell, Idaho: Caxton Printers, 1951. See also Prentice: *Farming for Famine*, p. 7f., Garden City, N. Y.: Doubleday, Doran, 1936. Prentice's data comes from Cornelius Walford: *The Famines of the World: Past and Present*, March 19, 1878, *Journal of the Royal Statistical Society*, vol. 41, p. 433; vol 42, p. 79.

[7] William T. Davis, editor: *Bradford's History of Plymouth Plantation*, 1606-1646, p. 146f. New York: Charles Scribner's Sons, 1908.

statist controls. As Montesquieu observed, "Countries are not cultivated in proportion to their fertility, but to their liberty."[8]

Not nature but man is the major cause of famine. Natural disasters such as storms, droughts, and frost can indeed destroy crops, but their effect is local, not total. Free production elsewhere can alleviate a shortage in a stricken area. In 1967, killing frosts in the San Jocquin Valley of California in some cases destroyed all the fruit on many farms. Farms sometimes within sight of a devastated farm came through the frost with minor damage. Some produce was in short supply, but other produce supplied the lack by bumper crops. Farmers whose crops were destroyed did not starve. Those who had savings used them to weather the year; many wives went to work to alleviate the financial crisis. The uses of freedom and industry saw these farmers through a crisis without any famine, nor with any proclamation of a national disaster calling for federal funds.

Walford listed, among the causes of famine, the following factors which are of particular significance:

1. The prevention of cultivation or the willful destruction of crops;
2. Defective agriculture caused by communistic control of land;
3. Governmental interference by regulation or taxation;
4. Currency restrictions, including debasing the coin.[9]

The world, during its least populous eras, suffered most from hunger and famine. As statist controls receded in the 19th century, hunger also began to recede, and Western civilization increasingly saw famine banished and hunger successfully dealt with. A far greater population enjoyed far greater supplies of food.

The reason for this increased supply of food was not simply technology nor the Industrial Revolution. The application of technology to Russian farming since 1917 has not seen an increase in the food supply. On the contrary, food production has declined, and the Ukraine, once the bread-basket of Europe, has been unable to feed the Soviet Union. Technology has not increased the food supply of Red China nor of any other Socialist regime. The reason

[8] Montesquieu: *Spirit of Laws*, Bk xviii, ch. 3.
[9] Cited by Prentice: *Hunger and History*, p. 4.

5

for the increased supply of food was the growth of freedom. Now "Thanks to Socialism, famine again stalks the earth. . . . Like a horse and carriage, 'socialism and hunger' inevitably go together." As a result, "Much of Eastern Europe, once a granary in its own right, lives off U. S. surpluses, while the fertile farmlands of Algeria, which produced so bountifully for the hard-working colons, have turned barren."[10] In the United States, as a result of the increasing socialistic controls of farming, food production is declining to the point that civil government officials can speak of future food problems, and a conservative writer can describe the policy as planned famine.[11]

The answer then to our problem is in essence this: socialism always creates ultimately an imbalance between the number of people living and their food supply which results in hunger or famine. There is in this sense therefore always a problem of over-population under socialism. Hunger is chronic and endemic to socialism.

Socialism, moreover, affects both the food supply, by limiting it, and also the population, by both expanding it at one stage and limiting it at another. Socialism grows in a country by catering to a group or to various groups by subsidies. These subsidies penalize the tax-payers for the benefit of favored groups who are termed "needy" but are now in actuality an undeservedly privileged group.

A subsidized group experiences a "population explosion." Being released from the responsibility of work, it lacks inhibitions and feels no constraint about rapid increase. Since more children may be a means of increased subsidy, the inhibition of financial accountability and responsibility is removed. Absorption with sex, and irresponsible sex, are products of a welfare economy. Zoo animals have a different sexuality than do wild animals.[12] A zoo is a welfare economy, and the zoo animals are privileged—and enslaved— animals. A welfare economics gives a privileged and enslaved status to a segment of the population. Again, America gives us a

10 "The Third Horseman: Thanks to Socialism, Famine Stalks the Earth," in *Barron's National Business and Financial Weekly,* December 20, 1965, p. 1.
11 Dan P. Van Gorder: *Ill Fares the Land.* Boston: Western Islands, 1968.
12 Robert Ardrey: *African Genesis,* p. 118. New York: Atheneum, 1961.

familiar and telling illustration. The American Negro, under slavery, existed in a welfare economy, because slavery is a form of welfare economics. The possession of slaves gave social status but it was not an economic asset. The slave gained cradle to grave security for a minimum of work. His living conditions were sometimes good and sometimes bad, but, on the whole, far superior to those of the peoples of Red China and the Soviet Union. A comparison of the census figures with respect to free and slave Negroes through 1860 is instructive:[13]

Census of—	Free colored	Increase, %	Slaves	Increase, %
1790	59,466	----	697,897	----
1800	108,395	82.28	893,041	29.97
1810	186,446	72.00	1,191,364	33.40
1820	233,524	25.33	1,538,038	28.79
1830	319,599	36.87	2,009,043	30.61
1840	386,303	20.87	2,487,455	23.81
1850	434,449	12.46	3,204,313	28.82
1860	482,122	10.97	3,953,587	23.38

These figures need qualification by a number of important facts. *First*, the slave population was at first increased by the importation of slaves, but Congress banned the slave trade in 1807, in terms of the Constitutional provision (Article 1, Section 9) which barred Congress from banning the importation of slaves prior to 1808, but made possible legislation thereafter. The number of slaves smuggled in thereafter was not great. *Second*, the slave population was regularly decreased by the freeing of slaves, and by the escaping of slaves. That this was a substantial decrease the table of "free colored" indicates. By 1860 one out of every eight Negroes in the United States was a free Negro, and this fact does not include Negroes who left slavery and America as well, to enter Canada, the West Indies, Liberia (by resettlement), and to join Indian tribes. *Third*, the slave Negro population was increased between 1849 and 1850 by the admission of Texas to the Union. The increase prior to the admission of these slaves was 23.81% and, a decade after the census of 1850, settled back again to 23.38%. Previous increases

[13] Joseph C. G. Kennedy, Sup't: *Preliminary Report on the Eighth Census*, 1860, p. 7. Washington: Government Printing Office, 1862.

7

were higher. Thus, with the various forms of losses included, it is clear that the slave birth rate was high. Comparison with the white birth rate prior to 1860 is difficult, because immigration added so heavily to the white population. The total population, inclusive of Negroes and immigrants, rose from 3,929,214, in 1790 to 31,443,321 in 1860. In 1860, the foreign born numbered 4,096,753, a high percentage; add to this their children, and those born of immigrants who had come earlier and died prior to the 1860 census, and the effect of immigration on the white census is marked.[14]

The "free colored" statistics are, *first*, given an artificial increase, i.e., one not dependent on birth rate, by the regular addition of freed slaves and escaped slaves. *Second*, as time went on, and the free Negro became a separate group whose increase became less dependent on the freeing of slaves owned by Northerners, the percentage of increase dropped markedly. *Third*, the birth rate for free Negroes was markedly lower than for slaves, and the death rate for free Negroes was markedly higher. Thus, in Boston, for the five-year period ending in 1859, the city registrar reported, "The number of colored births was one less than the number of marriages, and the deaths exceeded the births in the proportion of nearly two to one." In Philadelphia, for the last six months of 1860, there were "148 births against 306 deaths among the free colored." Town and country statistics were more favorable for the free Negro, but the mortality rate was still high, and in Rhode Island and Connecticut the deaths exceeded the births. The census report, surveying all areas, concluded, "In a simple statement, when viewed apart from the liberations or manumission in the Southern States, the aggregate free colored in this country must represent nearly what is termed 'a stationary population,' characterized by an equality of the current births and deaths."[15]

The Census of 1860 estimated that the total population of the United States would reach "about a hundred million" by 1900, but it estimated that, with emancipation likely, due to the start of the

[14] *The Statistical History of the United States from Colonial Times to the Present*, pp. 8, 11f. Stamford, Connecticut: Fairfield Publishers, 1965.
[15] *Eighth Census, 1860*, p. 6.

8

Civil War, "so many (Negroes) will be transferred from a faster to a slower rate of increase," that "nine millions of the colored, in the year 1900, appears a large estimate."[16] The Negro population in 1900 reached 8,833,994, the total population, 75,994,575. There was thus a marked decline in the ratio of the colored population after 36 years of freedom. Slavery, as a welfare economy, had encouraged the birth rate. The further the Negro left behind slavery and plantation patronage, the more his population statistics indicated a declining birth-rate. The following statistics are revealing:[17]

Year	White	Negro	Indian	Total
1860	26,922,537	4,441,830	44,021	31,443,321
1900	66,809,196	8,833,994	237,196	75,994,575
1930	110,286,740	11,891,143	332,397	122,775,046
1960	158,831,732	18,871,831	523,591	179,323,175

The above statistics do not list Chinese, Japanese, and other groups. The Indians are included to indicate that an Indian population greater than ever existed in pre-Columbian America now lives with millions of Americans without famine. Indian America was over-populated; modern white America is not.

The statistics are also important in that they show the marked decline in the ratio of Negroes to whites from 1860 to 1930; the Indians showed some increase in the same time, because the reservation system provided them with a welfare economy. The census of 1860 did not include Western Indians, but their numbers at that time were limited in the West. Their strong resistance has created the illusion of great numbers in men's minds. The Negro ratio declined to 1930 but returned to about the same ratio as 1860 in 1960. In other words, a generation of welfare, beginning with the New Deal of President Franklin Delano Roosevelt, provided a return to the subsidized conditions of the Negro of 1860.

Thus, a welfare economy, up to a point, increases a segment of the population. Whether in ancient Rome or modern America, this increase is of the worst segment of the population in ability, intelli-

[16] Ibid., p. 8.
[17] Ian Golenpaul, editor: Information Please Almanac, 1967, p. 324. New York: Simon and Schuster, 1966.

9

gence, and character. The worst elements of the Negro populations are subsidized to the detriment of the non-subsidized whites and Negroes. In 1965, in the cities, nearly one-fourth of Negro women who have been married were now divorced or separated as against a 7.9 per cent rate for white women. "Nearly one out of every four Negro babies born" was illegitimate, a Negro illegitimacy rate of 23.6 per cent as against a white rate of 3.07. More than half of all Negro children in 1965 were helped by federal-state Aid to Dependent Children, as against an 8 per cent rate for white children. The birth rate for Negroes was 40 per cent higher than for whites, so that it was estimated that by 1972 "Negroes will make up one-eighth of the U. S. population."[18] The situation since 1965 has become rapidly worse.

However, with full socialism, the need to gain votes by subsidy gives way to totalitarian controls over all the people, and population figures then show a frequent decline. Population figures for the U.S.S.R. are estimates only, in that the data is carefully guarded by that state, and the indications of population decline and famine are many.

The answer to the question, "What is over-population?" is that it is an imbalance between the number of people living and their food supply. This is a condition the world has faced during most of its history. As a result, we can answer the question, "Does the world face over-population?" that it indeed does face over-population, hunger, and famine progressively as it becomes more and more socialistic. Socialism has a poor record when it comes to eliminating problems: its answer adds up to eliminating people. In fact, one of socialism's major and chronic problems is simply *people*. Socialism on the one hand destroys production, and, on the other, breeds up the least desirable elements. Its answer is to find the people at fault. Socialism always faces over-population; a free economy does not.

---

[18] "Negro Revolt — The Big City Crisis," in San Francisco *Call-Bulletin*, Saturday, August 14, 1965, p. 2.

II

TOO MANY PEOPLE?

Socialism *decreases* production and it also causes a decline in the middle classes numerically by means of oppressive taxation; it is thus a means of population control with respect to the productive middle classes. On the other hand, socialism *increases* population among the lower classes by means of its welfare subsidies. Thus socialism has an immediate double impact on population. A third impact of socialism on population then becomes its effort to *control and limit* population. Very early in the modern socialist era, the sociologists began to realize that the worst element was the most prolific. Thus, by World War II, the figures of A. B. Hollingshead and W. L. Warner showed, as Marston Bates bluntly stated it, "The bums . . . were the most prolific," i.e., the lower-lower classes.[1]

Not surprisingly, the "scare headlines" began to stress over-population. Thus, we were told, "California's Population: 'Disaster Ahead.' " In fact, "If the present net gain of 1500 new residents daily continues, there will be 1½ billion people in California in 100 years, about half the present population of the entire planet."[2] Man, we are told, and by 'man' the state is meant, must control population growth.[3] In fact, one scientist is busy studying insects as food at the University of California at Riverside. Dr. Ronald L. Taylor urges the use of wax moth caterpillars, grasshoppers, bees, ants, grubs, wood lice, and termites "as an answer to the population explosion. He said that there is more protein potential in insects than

[1] Marston Bates: *The Prevalence of People*, p. 55. New York: Charles Scribner's Sons, 1955.

[2] Harrison Humphrey, "California's Population: 'Disaster Ahead,' " in Los Angeles *Herald-Examiner*, Sunday, June 19, 1966 p. 1.

[3] Joseph L. Myler "Man Must Control Population," Oakland, California, *Tribune*, Thursday, October 26, 1967, p. 25-F.

11

in cattle."[4] Our major problem, we are told, is people, too many of them. A Harvard researcher, Lincoln H. Day, of the Harvard School of Public Health, insist that big families are a threat to survival and that "American couples will have to limit their families to only two children to curb a 'runaway' population explosion which threatens to destroy the nation's 'quality of life.' "[6] The world is running out of food, we are also warned.[7] A food crisis is approaching.[8] The world's problem is too many people and too little food.[9] Famine stalks the earth, and it is insisted that the basic problem is a skyrocketing population that menaces the earth.[10] "Either man now turns his science and reason toward the problem of regulating excessive population growth—and nowhere is there evidence of such an intellectual redirection—or, prodigal in his procreation, he continues blithely on his way, increasingly injured by the mounting pressures of exploding populations."[11] The exploding population problem, if unchecked, dooms the United States to "a slow death."[12] Not only did many churches concern themselves with the problem, but tract racks began to carry a Hugh Moore Fund pamphlet, *The Population Bomb*. Within Roman Catholic circles the "problem" of over-population began to become a familiar refrain also. Catholic writers prepared a *National Review* Supplement on "The Population Explosion" demanding action.[13]

4 Dave Felton, "Caterpillars That Pop Like Corn Seen Feeding Soaring Population," Los Angeles *Times*, April 28, 1966.

5 Sid Moody, "People, People, People," in the San Francisco *Examiner*, Sunday, April 18, 1965, Section 1 p. A, 7; and the same article by Sid Moody, titled "Birth Rate World's Headache, Heartache," Oakland, California, *Tribune*, Sunday, April 18, 1965, p. 45.

6 Bill Martin "Big Families Held Threat to Survival," Oakland *Tribune*, Friday, April 2, 1965, p. 1.

7 F. J. Stare, M.D., "Food and Your Health: Too Many Mouths to Feed?" in Los Angeles *Times*, Monday, December 27, 1965, Part VIII, p. 2.

8 Louis Cassels, "World Food Crisis," in Los Angeles *Herald-Examiner*, Sunday, December 10, 1967, p. F4.

9 "Too Many People — Too Little Food," *United Business Service*, August 15, 1966, p. 323.

10 "Famine Stalks the Earth," full page advertisement by the Hugh Moore Fund, 60 East 42nd Street, New York, N. Y.10017, in *The Wall Street Journal*, Thursday, January 6, 1966, p. 11; Los Angeles.

11 Theodore Dohrman, "Populations in Underdeveloped Countries," in *Foreign Service Journal*, August, 1962, p. 23.

12 Al Martinez, "Population Boom — Is U.S. Doomed to Slow Death?" in Oakland *Tribune*, Tuesday, January 23, 1962, p. 2.

13 "The Population Explosion," Theodore Sturgeon, Pyrrho, Dr. Alan Guttmacher, Gary Wills, in *National Review*, vol. XVII, no. 30, July 27, 1965, pp. 633-648.

A publication of the San Antonio, Texas, Archdiocese, while rejecting the answers of abortion and birth control, also viewed the situation as one of grave over-population.[14]

Major periodicals regularly trumpet the menace. Thus we are warned:

> The current rate of growth, continued in 600 years, would leave every inhabitant of the world with only 1 square yard to live on. By the year 3500, the weight of human bodies on the earths surface would equal the weight of the world itself. By the year 6000, the solid mass of humanity would be expanding outward into space at the speed of light. "The world has cancer," a top Rockefeller Foundation official has said, "and that cancer cell is man."[15]

Other scientists give us similar statistical nightmares:

> A British scientist recently calculated that with the population of the world now about 3 billion and doubling every 37 years, we will reach the ultimate terrestrial limit of 60 million billion humans in somewhat less than 1,000 years. At that stage, people will be jammed together so tightly that the earth itself will glow orange-red from the heat.[16]

Doomsday is within the life-time of the younger generation, we are warned:

> London. (UPI) Jot down on the calendars for Nov. 13, 2026: Doomsday.
>
> And don't plan on heading for the hills then. An American scientist says there won't be any room.
>
> Dr. Robert White-Stevens, an American expert on fertilizers and insecticides, predicted here yesterday that, at present growth rates, the world by Nov. 13, 2026, will no longer be able to feed its population and will be stumbling all over itself.
>
> On that date, he said, the world's population will have reached 50 billion—a point where there are more mouths to feed than food available, and more bodies to house than land. He said there would be 10,000 persons in every square mile of land, including Antartica and the Sahara Desert.
>
> The American scientist said the world's ultimate practical population is

[14] "Debate Emerging in U.S. on Population Dilemma," in *The Alamo Messenger*, Friday, February 11, 1966, p. 3.

[15] "How Many Babies is Too Many?" in *Newsweek*, vol. LX, no. 4, July 23, 1962, p. 27.

[16] "Population Explosion and 'Anti-Babyism,'" Editorial, *Life*, vol. 58, no. 16, p. 6, April 23, 1965.

7 billion. Its current population of 3.2 billion is expanding by 7,000 persons a day, he noted.[17]

Another scientist, Dr. Albert Szent-Gyorgi, a Nobel Prize winner in 1937, has predicted, "If world population growth continues its ever-increasing pace, the time will come when 'men will have to kill and eat one another.' " His remarks were clearly aimed at theologians who challenge the population and birth control concepts:

> If human life is sacred and it is a sin to kill, extinguish a life, then it is an even greater sin to call into existence a human life without the ability or the desire to provide for it, leaving procreation to blind instincts, a burden on the rest of society.[18]

Another scientist, Dr. John R. Platt, has proposed contraceptive foods as a solution to the population "problem." By introducing agents in foodstuffs, the population could be controlled.

> "Any couple that really wanted to have a baby would have to go down the street and buy untreated food from the 'other store,' " he said. "But this wouldn't necessarily be a bad thing. It would mean 'every child a wanted child,' which would be a change of revolutionary value for the physical and psychological well-being of the children of the next generation."
>
> Such a population control effort is beyond reach technically as well as politically at the moment.
>
> But Platt told the American Institute of Planners the process, once perfected, could be as simple as putting vitamin D in milk or adding iodine to salt.[19]

Another scientist has called for mass temporary sterilization of all women:

> Hamilton, Ont. Dec. 12 (AP). Dr. William Bradford Shockley, who shared a Nobel Prize in 1956 for helping to develop the transistor, has proposed a sweeping birth control plan that includes temporary sterilization of all women and government approval before each baby.

[17] White-Stevens is a senior scientific expert at the Cyanamid Agricultural Research Center in New Jersey. "Scientist Pegs Doomsday," Oakland *Tribune*, Wednesday, August 31, 1966, p. E-19.

[18] Rudy Abramson, "Scientist's Warning: Population Rise May Produce Cannibalism," Los Angeles *Times*, Thursday, January 20, 1966, Part I p. 2. This scientist's reference to "blind instincts" is a curious one; scientific evidence seems to indicate a very great ability on the instinctual level which can hardly be called "blind." His reference, of course, is not to instincts but to sexual drives.

[19] Rudy Abramson, "Contraceptive Food May Curb Population," Los Angeles *Times*, Tuesday, October 3, 1967, Part 1, p. 7.

The Stanford University physicist explained his plan in a lecture at McMaster University last night and also accused "inverted liberals" of blocking research into inherited intelligence differences between Negroes and whites.

The chief points of Shockley's birth control plan are these:

The public would first of all vote on the rate of population growth it wants. The Census Bureau would determine how many children each couple could have in keeping with the predetermined growth rate and certificates would be issued to them.

All girls would be temporarily sterilized by time-capsule contraceptives. When a woman and her husband wanted children, they would have the time capsule removed by a public health agency on turning in one of their certificates. After the child was born, the contraceptive capsule would be reinserted.

Couples not wishing children or wishing less than they were entitled to could sell their surplus certificates on the open market.

Under this system, Shockley said, "only people who want and can afford children will have them."

The physicist also made a plea for research into racial differences. . . .[20]

Shockley's assumption is that the right to give birth, and the number of children one can have, is subject to the ballot. What then will prevent the majority from denying the right of birth to minority groups?

Still another scientist blamed the family for society's discontents. While his remarks were not directed towards the population problem, they were in accord with the general attack on the family as a source of social ills which include over-population.

London (AP). A British social anthropologist said yesterday "the family" and the older generation are the root of society's discontents.

"Far from being the basis of the good society, the family with its narrow privacy and tawdry secrets is the source of all our discontents," said Edmund Leach, provost of King's College, Cambridge.

[20] "Sweeping New Birth Control Proposal," Los Angeles *Herald-Examiner*, Tuesday, December 12, 1967, p. A-18. See also San Jose, California, *Mercury*, "Nobel Laureates in Dispute Over Government Birth Curb," Tuesday, January 10, 1967, p. 13. Shockley, according to this report, stated that "The whole concept of 'bad heredity' is in any case a myopic one, since the high values of one social milieu are the vices of another one and our milieu is constantly changing." Shockley proposed, as an experiment to test his theories, putting adopted Negro children in white families to measure relative effects of heredity and environment.

"The family looks inward upon itself, there is an intensification of emotional stress between husband and wife, and parents and children."

He spoke in a lecture broadcast by the British Broadcasting Corp.

Defending the young people of today, Leach said society had failed to create a world fit for young people to live in and this failure was marked by "rapid hostility" toward the young. . . ."[21]

Radical solutions abound for the problem of over-population, and the family is given little respect in the considerations. The family increasingly is seen as an enemy to survival "in a rapidly moving world." This means that the family resists social planning.[22]

The situation, we are warned, is very grave. Pendell gives us a graphic summary statement of the matter:

The hell they brew by two and two is hell for me and hell for You! POPULATION ON THE LOOSE MEANS REPRODUCTION UN-RESTRAINED

Earth's area is finite: man's reproductive power is infinite.

If 1% more people would add less than 1% more product, overpopulation exists. To exploit all our resources now is to eat a week's rations in one day—and then go hungry!

As a rule, the fewer qualifications people have for parenthood the more children they have

Civilizations collapse because problem makers multiply faster than problem solvers

Our own civilization must end if average heredity continues to weaken

Reproduction is something that can easily be overdone.

Quality of men; quality of earth: harmony between men's numbers and earth's abundance—for these we strive

The misguidance of COUPLES has resulted in the calamities of NATIONS

One characteristic of Catholic countries is gnawing hunger

Population conditions, worldwide in their problem aspects, have their cause in the behavior of pairs

[21] "Sociologist Raps Familial Society." Oakland *Tribune*, Monday, November 27, 1967, p. 5.

[22] "The People Crisis: It's a Brave New . . . What?" Los Angeles *Herald-Examiner*, Sunday, December 11, 1966, Section G, p. 1.

> Only population control can keep any country's numbers right, or the quality of its citizens high[23]

Pendell asked for drastic action, including mass sterilization of people on the lower level: "begin at the bottom; sterilize far enough up the quality scale to make the quantity no greater than is appropriate for the long-run drag on food resources."[24] Marriage should not be permitted, according to Pendell, without an I.Q. test, a passing grade of 90 or more being required for a marriage license. Persons having hereditary defects should also be barred from marrying.[25] Artificial insemination should be used to increase the quality of the human breed.[26]

The problem is intensified, we are told, by the "fact" that "population is, indeed, a nation's greatest resource," and great numbers mean great power.[27] Because the population growth is ostensibly in the East, the Organski's hold that "World power, then, is passing from the West, for the largest nations lie in the East. If, as seems likely, these lands complete their own industrialization successfully, their size alone guarantees to them a place that Western nations cannot rival."[28] From this perspective, it is numbers plus state planned industrialization that equals greatness. This is materialism with a vengeance.

Others hold, as for example, Hauser, that a limitation of population is necessary if the West, and the United States, is to maintain its quality and power.[29] The ratio of population to arable land is an increasingly unfavorable one which is productive of famine.[30] The time has come, we are told, to raise the question "What right have you to have a child?"[31] When World War II ended, Vogt urged

---

[23] Elmer Pendell: *Population on the Loose*, p. vii. New York. Wilfred Funk, 1951.

[24] *Ibid.*, p. 324.

[25] *Ibid.*, p. 333f.

[26] *Ibid.*, p. 340ff.

[27] Katherine Organski and A. F. K. Organski: *Population and World Power*, p. 3. Knopf, 1961.

[28] *Ibid.*, p. 251.

[29] Philip M. Hauser: *Population Perspectives*, pp. 157ff. New Brunswick, New Jersey: Rutgers University Press, 1960.

[30] Fairfield Osborn: *Our Plundered Planet*, p. 37. New York: Grosset & Dunlap, 1948.

[31] William Vogt: *People! Challenge to Survival*, pp. 150ff. New York: William Sloane Associates, 1960.

a foreign aid program contingent upon "population stabilization through *voluntary* action of the people."[32]

Since we are so firmly assured that we are in the midst of a population explosion, can we assume that firm statistical evidence abounds to document this claim? After all, the term "population explosion" is a highly emotional one, and one would assume that the scientists are on firm ground in using a scare phrase. Marston Bates observed:

> The statistics are not exact, of course. There is no way of registering the daily births and deaths for much of Asia, Africa, and South America. But the experts are in close agreement about the figures. . . .[33]

This is good science, of course; where there are no registers of births and deaths, we are still given detailed population statistics! The experts agree with one another, but do they agree with reality?

The population figures, as reported by these experts, are extensive and full for the entire world. Footnotes indicate that full data is often unobtainable, but the total impression is of a reliable, scientific report.[34] On the basis of this vast network of guesswork, projections are also made of future population growth.[35] The forecasting is based on a minimal amount of data. Stanbery and Hermann are correct in stating that "Population forecasting is essentially a matter of judgment."[36] Among the many presuppositions of a non-statistical character which go into forecasting are the following "basic assumptions implicit in all forecasts":

> The form of government and the political, economic, and social organization and institutions of the United States will remain substantially unchanged.

[32] William Vogt: *Road to Survival*, p. 211. New York: William Sloane Associates, 1948.

[33] Marston Bates: *Expanding Population in a Shrinking World*, p. 1. New York: American Library Association and Public Affairs Pamphlets, 1963.

[34] See, for example, Statistical Office of the United Nations, Department of Economic and Social Affairs: *Demographic Yearbook 1965*. New York: United Nations, 1966.

[35] See National Planning Association, Bureau of Labor Statistics, U. S. Department of Labor: *Projections to the Year 1976 and 2000: Economic Growth, Population, Labor Force and Leisure, and Transportation*, ORRRC Report no. 23, Washington, D.C., 1962; see also U. N. Department of Economic and Social Affairs, Population Studies, no. 41: *World Population Prospects as Assessed in 1963*. New York: United Nations, 1966.

[36] Van Bueren Stanbery and Frank V. Hermann: *Population Forecasting Methods*, p. 6. Revision of June, 1964 by Hermann of Stanberys study of 1952. U. S. Dept. of Commerce, Bureau of Public Roads, Urban Planning Division.

No all-out war, internal revolution, nationwide devastation, epidemic, or other disaster will occur.

No large-scale epidemic, destruction by military action, fire, earthquake, or other disaster will occur in the area or within the geographical or economic region to which the area is closely related.

Any of these events might have completely unpredictable effects on the population. These basic assumptions, therefore, are either explicitly stated or are implied in nearly every population projection.[37]

These "basic assumptions" are truly remarkable ones. They assume that man has now conquered all the major problems of man, history, and nature and can thus proceed in terms of an assured clear sailing. The basic assumption is that we are now on the verge of utopia.

We are told that, until now, man has had serious natural checks on his birth rate which led to a high mortality rate and checked population. According to Dorn, "Through the centuries of his existence man undoubtedly has had a birth rate which, if unchecked, long ago would have led to standing room only in the world."[38] Deevey has observed, of world population figures, "One suspects that writers have been copying each other's guesses."[39]

We are told that man now has a longer life-expectancy and thus a higher breeding potential. Here as elsewhere the facts are loosely used. The conquest is largely of childhood diseases, not of diseases of maturity to the same degree. In the United States, in 1900 a new-born child had a life expectancy of 48 years, but by 1950, the expectancy had increased to 67 years, ostensibly a gain of 19 years. But this is only part of the story. In 1900, the life expectancy of a man of 50 was 21 years, i.e., to 71, and in 1950, it was 22 years, a gain of only one year.[40] Another question arises: by keeping more weaker babies alive, are we potentially weakening the life-expectancy of adults of tomorrow by perpetuating weaker strains?

Another neglected factor is urbanization. City life in the long

[37] *Ibid.*, p. 7f.

[38] Harold F. Dorn, "World Population Growth," in The American Assembly, Columbia University: *The Population Dilemma*. Englewood Cliffs, New Jersey: Prentice-Hall, 1963.

[39] Edward S. Deevey, Jr., "The Human Population," *Scientific American*, September, 1960, reprint, p. 5.

[40] J. L. Rodale: *Are We Really Living Longer?* Emmaus, Pennsylvania: Rodale Books, 1955.

run has a depressing effect on the birth rate and apparently on virility. According to Thompson, "The big mononucleated city is doing things to our reproductive life the significance of which we realize only dimly as yet."[41] In a study of London, Sinclair reported:

> Havelock Ellis, suggesting that "a great metropolis swiftly kills those whom it attracts," tells how Cantlie fifty years ago defined a Londoner as one whose parents and grandparents were born and bred in London; "but during the four years in which he investigated this question he was unable to find a single Londoner in this true and definite sense, and even those who were Londoners back to the grandparents on one side only were unusually stunted or feeble, or unlikely to propagate. Dr. Harry Campbell . . . , among two hundred London-born children, found two or three whose parents and grandparents were born and bred in London, and these children were very delicate." The late George Russell ("A.E.") interested in the same phenomenon, was able to find only one person who was a fourth-generation Londoner.[42]

Studies do indicate that population density leads to social pathology and a decline in fertility. There is thus some indication that the growth of cities may lead naturally to a declining birth rate.[43] Tentative evidence suggests that mental stress has an effect on the birth rate.[44]

The Soviet Union has long had a problem with a low birth rate, and census data is not freely released, nor is published information trustworthy. The low birth rate led to payments for births to increase the birth rate. Payments were set to begin with the third child:

> The estimated annual wage in Russia was 4,020 rubles for 1940, so a woman having a child every year received, for her 7th and subsequent children more than her average worker husband received for his work.
>
> However, she can't stop having children, because if she does, the down payments cease at once and the flow of income stops after four years.[45]

Since then, there has been no change of any significant sort in the

[41] Warren S. Thompson: *Population Problems*, p. 339. New York: McGraw-Hill, 1942.
[42] Robert Sinclair: *The Big City, A Human Study of London*, p. 36f. American edition. New York: Reynal & Hitchcock, 1938.
[43] See John B. Calhoun, "Population Density and Social Pathology," pp. 139ff. *Scientific American*, vol. 206, no. 2, February, 1962.
[44] Deevey, *loc cit*.
[45] Pendell: *Population on the Loose*, p. 171.

declining birth rate, according to all indications.[46] Socialist life does not apparently promote fertility.

France also is again concerned with a declining birth rate.[47] Australia's birth rate is also declining and Australians are "wooing Europeans and Americans to come to their country—they offer to pay 90% of the fare."[48] Ronald Freedman, director of the University of Michigan Population Studies Centre, has predicted a "major decline in birth rates" for much of Asia and cited evidence that it was already under way.[49]

In the United States, in 1966, a nine year decline of 24 per cent was reported and showed signs of continuing to decline.[50] The decline continued in 1967.[51] According to one headline, "U. S. Birth Rate Sputters Out."[52] As a result, revised estimates of future population statistics began to appear.[53]

Canada also experienced a marked decline in its birth rate.[54]

Population figures are lacking in Black Africa, but the indications are that the break-up of tribal life is having a radical effect on the family which is likely to affect the birth rate.

> Urbanism creates another problem—a brand-new one.

> In 1939 less than 10 percent of the people in Africa lived in cities. Today approximately 30 percent are urban dwellers. More than 70 percent of the rural men have left for urban areas. Demographers predict that at least 75 percent of the population will soon be urbanized.

[46] James W. Bracket: *Projections of the Population of the U.S.S.R., By Age and Sex:* 1964-1985, U. S. Dept. of Commerce, Bureau of the Census, International Population Reports, Series P-91, No. 13; 1964. See also Edmond Le Breton, "Soviet Birth Rate Drops," Palo Alto, California, *Times*, Monday July 5, 1965 p. 23; "Communist Birth Control" *Parade's* "Intelligence Report," March 26, 1967, p. 26.

[47] "France Worried Over Declining Birth Rate," Los Angeles *Times*, Monday, December 4, 1967, Part VII, p. 8.

[48] *Parade*, "Intelligence Report," July 11, 1965, p. 16.

[49] "Professor sees decline in Asian birth rates," *Hong Kong Tiger Standard*, Sunday, April 25, 1965, p. 1.

[50] "Birth Control Going Too Far in the U. S.?" *U. S. News & World Report*, May 9, 1966, pp. 44-46.

[51] "U. S. Birth Rate Still Declining," Santa Ana *Register*, Thursday (m), March 30, 1967, p. A-19.

[52] San Francisco *Examiner*, Sunday, March 14, 1965, Section II, p. 8.

[53] See *U. S. News & World Report*, "What's Ahead in the Population Boom," May 6, 1963, pp. 68-71; "As Family Planning Gains Favor in U. S.," January 9, 1967, pp. 48-50; "No More Population Explosion for the U. S.?" April 17, 1967, pp. 48-50.

[54] "Down, Down Goes the Birth Rate, And Canada Is Feeling the Effects." *National Observer*, February 27, 1967, p. 6.

> Statistics cannot show the moral and family breakdown that accompanies this shift; but the urban masses are rootless.[55]

But a declining birth rate does not necessarily mean a declining population. According to Leo Cherne, for the United States to achieve a static population, "the birth rate would have to be one-half what it is now."[56]

The alarmists thus feel our problem is still grave and needs radical solutions. Thus, Dr. Paul Ehrlich of Stanford University proposed limiting the U. S. population to 150 million, 50 million fewer than at present. This requires compulsory controls to limit birth.[57]

The question thus must be raised: what controls birth? A variety of answers have been given. Zoologists now point out that animal fertility declines automatically after a certain density is reached.[58] Is this operative in man?

The answer of Thomas Robert Malthus (1766-1834) to this question was both highly *rationalistic and biological.* Malthus was not new in his propositions.[59] He summed up effectively the Enlightenment approach to the subject of population. His conclusion, as he stated it, was this:

> Must it not then be acknowledged by an attentive examiner of the histories of mankind, that, in every age and in every state in which man has existed or does now exist, . . . The increase of population is necessarily limited by the means of subsistence; . . . Population invariably increases when the means of subsistence increase, unless prevented by powerful and obvious checks; . . . These checks, and the checks which keep the population down to the level of the means of subsistence, are moral restraint, vice, and misery?[60]

In the perspective of Malthus, man is basically driven by sexual drive to reproduce, and essentially only the lack of means of sub-

[55] Walter R. Beach, "Whither Africa," *Signs of the Times,* vol. 92, no. 9, September, 1965, p. 19f.

[56] Interview with Leo Cherne, "Birth Rate Up or Down?" *This Week,* Sunday, May 22, 1966, p. 2.

[57] "150 Million Census Lid Proposed," Oakland *Tribune,* Friday, November 17, 1967, p. 10.

[58] *Parade,* "Intelligence Report: Animal Population Control," March 5, 1967, p. 23..

[59] See Kenneth Smith: *The Malthusian Controversy.* London: Routledge & Kegan Paul, 1951.

[60] T. R. Malthus: *An Essay on Population,* vol. 1, p. 314f. Everyman's Library, 692. London: J. M. Dent.

sistence limits population. Malthus saw man as lacking in other than biological drives; the limitations on man are in almost all cases simply materialistic. In this respect, Malthus was biological in his theory. He was rationalistic, as all scientism is, in that he limited the causal factors to those which are rationally respectable and scientifically amenable.

Marx and Engels were profoundly influenced by Malthus, in that Darwin applied to the problem of origins Malthus' theory of the survival of the fittest and biological causality. But Marx and Engels rejected Malthus, because they felt his theory of population favored the capitalist in survival against the worker. In 1844, in his *Outlines of a Critique of Political Economy*, Engels wrote on "The Myth of Over-population."[61] Marx and Engels at this point wanted a social theory of overpopulation, not a biological one. Man, capitalist economics, was responsible for famine and starvation, not nature. Distribution rather than supply was the problem.

In 1822 Francis Place offered an answer to the "problem" of over-population which caught the crusading fervor of many liberals in the next century and half, birth control.[62]

The biological answer sees man mainly in terms of his reproductive drive. For these alarmists, reproduction is the enemy, and they outdo all ascetics in their horror of its power. "The whole structure is threatened by human reproduction, which for the most part has remained a force as uncivilized as fire in a factory or water in a surging flood."[63] Biologically, mice are capable of multiplying so rapidly that in a few months or years they could cover the earth to a depth of six feet, and oysters could also do the same, and many other creatures as well. But they do not. And man has not always increased and multiplied to the capacity of his subsistence; he has often declined in the face of it.

[61] Ronald L. Meek, editor: *Marx and Engels on Malthus*, pp. 57-63. London: Lawrence and Weshart, 1953, paperback edition, International Publishers, New York, 1954.

[62] Francis Place: *Illustrations and Proofs of the Principle of Population*, edited by Norman E. Hines. London: George Allen & Unwin, 1930.

[63] Pendell: *Population on the Loose*, p. 72. There is no lack of unconscious humor in these writers also; thus, one of the best, Marston Bates, in *The Prevalence of People*, begins his second paragraph of Chapter 6, on "Human Reproduction," with this important word: "Reproduction involves sex. . . ." (p. 80), an exciting bit of scientific reporting for all readers!

Moreover, while it is clearly true that people are in some areas over-crowded, it is also true that such over-crowing has existed more than once in history for a variety of reasons. We are told that "A million people do sleep on the streets of Calcutta and people do live on a mountain of garbage outside Lima."[64] But people often congregate for sociological reasons, i.e., overcrowding has often psychological and cultural roots, economic roots, and is not merely a problem of over-breeding. India, for example, has a religious problem above all else. Because of its unwillingness to kill animal life, India is over-populated with animals which are crowding out man. The sacred cows are a familiar fact, but rats are said to number 2.5 billion and they consume more than 875 million bushels of cereal grain annually, more than the United States could ship to them during 1966. "An additional 25 per cent of India's grain is lost thru defective storage, transport, handling, and processing facilities."[65]

It is true also that our natural resources are being laid waste and polluted. McClane noted,

> Our basic problem right now is that more than 50 percent of the American people are crowded into 1½% of our land and for the most part in areas with no semblance of community planning. . . . Indirectly our oceans are slowly dying from malnutrition. . . .[66]

But is this a product of over-population as such or of a profoundly false view of man's relationship to the world around him? More than once, a single miner has thoroughly polluted a stream without an assist from over-population. On the other hand, one major city, instead of polluting its land and waters with waste, is turning garbage into highly profitable fertilizer.

Whether men and nations use and develop the earth or abuse and lay waste its resources is essentially a moral question; not a matter of over-population. Japan and the Netherlands have had a long

[64] Sidney Moody, "Population Explosion Crisis Conjectural," in Oakland *Tribune*, Sunday, April 25, 1965, p. 47.

[65] Editorial "Let's Try Rat Poison!!" from the Cincinnati *Enquirer*, in the Chicago *Tribune*, Thursday, March 24, 1966.

[66] A. J. McClane, "Where Do We Go From Here?" *Field & Stream*, February, 1967, vol. LXXI, no. 16, pp. 12, 127.

history of high population density combined with an effective and wise use of natural resources. Only lately are they showing signs of moral dereliction here.

Instead of being over-populated, Dr. Karl Brandt has spoken of our serious underpopulation "by any standards we can reasonably apply. This country will not be overpopulated with 350,000,000 or many more people and will have a much higher standard of living."[67]

A geographer, Dr. George F. Carter, feels that population "experts" are talking nonsense when they speak of over-population:

> First, let's consider how we are actually using our space. In the United State in the last census decade (1950-1960) one-half of all the counties in the United States lost population. . . . Men are leaving the land and pouring into the cities. . . .
>
> Scotland is emptying out and the wild moors are wilder than ever. The Hebrides now have many uninhabited islands—islands where men have lived for more than 5,000 years. Ireland has half as many people as 100 years ago. Yucatan 500 years ago may have had several 100 people per square mile, but now has 1 per square mile. So, stop worrying so much about open spaces. We have more, not less than we had 100 years ago and we have better means of getting there in case you really crave the quiet of the wilderness. . . .
>
> Since 1957 the birth rate in the United States has declined every year. Should this trend continue, by the year 2000 deaths will outnumber births. Such things are possible. For instance, in Vienna, Austria today, deaths are exceeding births at a rate of two to one. Every country in Europe, except seven, is failing to produce sufficient children to replace the adult population. Suppression of such facts amounts to scandalous treatment of the data on population.
>
> . . . India is not overcrowded by other nations' standards: India— 300 per square mile, England—600, and Holland—800. If we want to play with figures, we can. These indicate that the more people you have per square mile the more prosperous you are and there is some truth to this.[68]

In many rural areas, especially in the eastern states, wild animals are making a strong come-back, and animals once believed to be extinct are re-appearing.

[67] "Man: Resource of Resources," *The National Observer*, July 15, 1963, p. 12.

[68] George F. Carter: *Are Population 'Experts' Running Wild?* pp. 6, 7, 10, 11. Huntington, Indiana: Our Sunday Visitor, pamphlet no. 84.

Norris, in calling attention to the declining birth rate, wrote in early 1967, "Here in Oxnard, Calif., it appears that the birth rate has dropped nearly forty percent in the past five years, and there are indications that it may drop even further this year."[69]

In view of these things, we are entitled to ask some questions:

Why is this myth of overpopulation so vigorously promoted? What is involved in assuming that these "experts" are right?

What governs population increase and decrease? Are there governing factors which are neglected by the proponents of the myth?

[69] Murray Norris, "The Myth of Overpopulation," *The Wanderer*, January 12, 1967, p. 5.

III

THE ECONOMICS OF POPULATION CONTROL

From one perspective, it can be argued that the title of this chapter is clearly wrong, that, instead of *economics*, it should read "The *Politics* of Population Control." Clearly, it is political action that is involved, political action by the state to control population through one means or another. By means of legislation and force, the state exercises its power over the population to control their behavior and their rate of birth.

On the other hand, the behavior of the state, while obviously *political* action, increasingly constitutes its *economic* program. The failure of the socialist state to control the economic order successfully and productively leads to a continual and inescapable economic crisis. The socialist state is less and less able to feed its people, less and less able to govern production successfully, and therefore increasingly unable to institute economic planning which has any reasonable correspondence to reality. This is the area of first effort, to control *production* and to direct it to a planned goal. But *production* and the *plan* fail to correspond. The *plan* can be altered and often is, without appreciable results, but the fact of *planning* is not altered or abandoned. Thus, two basic ingredients of the socialist order, the *plan or planning*, and *production*, reach a stalemate. Every effort to increase production continues to be made, but attention is given also to the third area, *consumption*. Consumption, like production, is already controlled, but it becomes subject to further controls. If the supply of food and materials is insufficient, if production fails to meet the demands by consumers, it is not the plan but the consumers who are at fault. As a result, the consumers must be controlled still further. Consumer control thus becomes a basic part of the plan in the socialist state.

The control of the consumer takes several directions. *First,* the control of *money* is basic to the control of the consumers, of the people. Money being the life-blood of the economic system, the control of money means that the economic life of the people is controlled. It is popular, in prosperous times, for otherwise intelligent men to remark foolishly that "you can't eat gold," but it needs to be observed by way of answer that you can't eat very long without it. Money buys food, and very few can hope to exist long without money to feed themselves. Real money is gold and silver; paper money is check-book money at best. Just as a check reads, "Pay to the order of . . . ," so valid paper money reads, "Payable to the bearer on demand" a specified sum in gold or silver. A person who issues checks beyond his ability to pay is guilty of fraud. A state which issues paper money beyond its gold and silver reserves is similarly guilty of fraud. The state, moreover, has the power to force its citizen-victims to accept the fraud. Total control of a people is possible through control of money, and, after World War II, the United States used special issues of paper currencies, made obligatory and mandatory in occupied Central Europe, its means of total control with a minimum of effort.[1]

Socialist orders, planning states, are thus entirely favorable to a purely fiat currency, to an unbacked paper money. Without such a monetary system, their totalitarian power is broken, since gold and silver make possible an independent wealth, since their intrinsic worth escapes the control of the state and the effort of the state to make itself the sole source of value.

Speaking before the Financial Conference of the National Industrial Conference Board in New York, February 14, 1968, William McChesney Martin, Jr., Chairman, Board of Governors of the Federal Reserve System, declared,

I have been quoted as saying that gold is a barbarous metal. But it

[1] Vladimir Petrov: *Money and Conquest, Allied Occupation Currencies in World War II.* Baltimore: The Johns Hopkins Press, 1967.

28

is not *gold* that is barbarous; that wasn't my point. Quite the contrary; gold is a beautiful and noble metal. What *is* barbarous, when it occurs, is man's enslavement to gold for monetary purposes.[2]

From Martin's perspective, gold is *barbarous* as the monetary standard. His use of the term *barbarous* is both revealing and a knowledgeable use. The word comes from the Latin *barbarus,* which was derived from the Greek *barbaros*, which had the connotation of both "foreign" and "slavish." Martin used it in the latter sense. For Martin, gold is enslaving, and he speaks of "man's enslavement to gold for monetary purposes," because for Martin freedom is slavery, and slavery is freedom. Gold frees the individual from the arbitrary paper money of the state, and paper money frees the state from the control of the people and places the people in the state's power. Gold enslaves the state to fiscal responsibility, but the modern state wants essentially a free state and a slave people. Gold is a roadblock to this goal.

The *second* means of controlling the population is also an economic means of control, wage and price controls. A traveller to the Soviet Union in 1967 observed:

> Rents for executives in the Government run from $6 to $16 a month. On the other hand one can very easily spend $6 for a single meal in the evening—namely, one month's rent.

> Jet fuel is sold within Russia at $3.50 a ton and aviation gasoline at $4.50 a ton. On the other hand, a white shirt costs $12. How can one equate this kind of economy to American standards? It's impossible.[3]

By controlling prices totally, the Socialist state controls the population. It can make its production largely unavailable by pricing its goods beyond the ability of the people to buy. Cars, shirts, jewelry, anything the state cannot produce, can be priced out of reach, and the limited production is matched to a now limited consumption. In the Soviet Union, income taxes are not necessary; total control of wages and prices makes such a step unnecessary, as does a fiat currency, which is in itself a form of income and inheri-

[2] William McC. Martin, Jr., "The Price of Gold is not the Problem," in *Federal Reserve Bulletin,* February, 1968, p. 120.

[3] "A Businessman Sizes Up Russia, Interview with a Management Authority" (Richard S. Morse), in *U. S. News & World Report,* vol. LXIII, no. 7, August 14, 1967, p. 51.

tance control. The wage controls give the state power to manipulate the population; wages can be increased to encourage the people, and prices also increased to limit their spending power. Through wage and price controls, the planners are able to correlate production and consumption a little more effectively. As a result, wage and price controls become a necessary instrument of population control. The people, with their unpredictable and unplanned desires (i.e., not planned by a central agency), upset socialist calculations. Because the principle of planning is assumed to be correct, the answer is that the selfish consumption of the people is to blame for the economic crisis caused by the failure of the plan. The result is wage and price controls, plus a program of "re-educating" the people.

But the crisis of socialism deepens. The economic control of the population by means of controlling production and consumption is not enough. As a result, a *third* instrument becomes necessary, *birth control* in the broadest sense, the control of the producers' and consumers' birth. It is commonly assumed that birth control is primarily a personal and familial matter, but such an assumption sees the situation without reference to the political order. Ideally, birth control is a personal and private concern, a moral decision for each couple to make. Realistically, it is now essentially a political concern, a basic tool in the economics of population control. Directly or indirectly, a major part of the research and propaganda is financed by the state and the results are then publicized by the state.[4]

Control of births by state action is not new, no more than pollution and depletion of natural resources. Man's abuse of the earth rests on an irreligious exploitation of it, and it is no less common in simpler cultures, sometimes more common, than in advanced ones. Thus, we read concerning Laos:

> The New York State Air Pollution Control Board's *Progress Report* announced that there is a semi-permanent inversion over a large segment of Laos.
>
> Mountain farmers, having exhausted one piece of land, can do nothing

[4] For a survey of the literature, see *A Survey of Research on Reproduction Related to Birth and Population Control* (as of January 1, 1963), 248ff., U. S. Department of Health, Education, and Welfare, Public Health Service, National Institute of Health, Public Health Service Publication No. 1066.

but burn off another patch of jungle. As a result the smoke gets thicker until, just before the summer monsoon knocks it down, it often extends up to 10,000 feet, with visibility seldom over 3,000.[5]

The so-called noble Greeks, long before Plato and Aristotle, had stripped Greece of its fine forests, and Greece's problem then was not too many people but too wrong a faith. All the same, because Plato's perspective was statist, his planning for man included population control by means of birth regulations. Only people within certain age groups (women between 20 and 40, men between 25 and 55) were to be permitted to have children; children born out of those years were to be disposed of, if not previously aborted.[6] Plato did not foresee a problem of over-population; his concern was with the power of the state to plan totally. The right to bear children was thus seen as totally within the state's jurisdiction and a legitimate area of state planning, since the children are being reared "for the state."[7] Thus, long before over-population was ever heard of, population control by means of restrictions on birth was a part of social planning. The rise of Christianity forced the abandonment of all such controls, but, in recent years, the aggressive revival of humanism has again made such controls on births a major factor in planning.

We are indeed assured that world socialization will give us effective population planning. According to a United Nations agency, "A new process is about to begin, or has perhaps already started, and the first signs of that 'socialization' of the world which appear on the horizon may be significant in this connexion."[8]

A group of American scientists, in research sponsored by the American Academy of Arts and Sciences, Cambridge, Mass., with the support of the Carnegie Corporation, have predicted, for "the year 2000, the millenium," the "decline of the family and of woman's

[5] "Pollution in Jungles," in *Natural Food News*, Atlanta, Texas, Vol. 5, no. 12, p. 8.
[6] *The Republic of Plato*, Bk. V, 461.
[7] *Ibid.*

[8] ST/SOA/Series A/28, *The Future Growth of World Population*, preface, v, Population Studies, no. 28. U. N. Dept. of Economics and Social Welfare, New York, 1958. On p. 24, we are told that, "Early in the century there was one European for every two Asians; by the end of the century, this ratio may have become one to four."

place in the home—except for those couples designated to breed children."[9] According to another report,

> The married couple of the future may need a special permit to have children, according to H. Bentley Glass, professor of biology at Johns Hopkins University.
>
> Penalty for having an illegitimate or unlicensed child should be sterilization, he said.
>
> "The right to have children can't remain unlimited," Dr. Glass said Tuesday at County Museum. "This is because the increase in world population is the second most serious threat to mankind. The most serious is nuclear war."
>
> Dr. Glass, in an interview before giving the last of the spring lectures sponsored by the museum's Science and History Alliance, said permits for a first and second child would be easy to get from the licensing agency.
>
> If a couple passed they would be issued a marriage license. The right to the first child would be automatic, and the family would even get a tax exemption.
>
> A second child would be licensed, too, although there would not be a second exemption. Instead of gaining an exemption for a third child, even if licensed, a couple would have $600 added to their taxable income.
>
> Dr. Glass said penalties for producing an unlicensed baby would be severe. He suggested sterilization as a punishment to fit the crime.
>
> The time may even come when reproduction is entirely separated from sex, with both sperm and ova kept in laboratories and matched up there by technicians.
>
> "I do not advocate this," Dr. Glass said, "but it is a possible or probable development."
>
> He predicted that the grosser differences among men, such as racial coloring, will disappear within the next 2,000 years or so, but that individual differences will remain.
>
> "The Negro population within the United States is probably already 30 percent white, and will disappear entirely," he said.[10]

[9] Andrew Squibb Jr., "The Year 2000," in Los Angeles *Herald-Examiner CALIFORNIA LIVING*, January 21, 1968, p. 4.

[10] George Getze, "Special Permit to Have Children Seen as Future Population Control," in Los Angeles *Times*, June 3, 1964, cited in *Prophetic Herald*, vol. 26, no. 5, May, 1965 p. 24.

Plans for such radical control of population appear widely, in the press, in scientific journals, and in popular periodicals. The people are steadily being prepared to believe that there is an over-population problem, and that radical controls are necessary. Thus, Dr. Sam McClatchie, M.D., believes that "Social Man" must face radical and total control by the state, the United Nations specifically, over birth. The scientific means for such control are very nearly available, we are told; vaccination against conception:

> I am presuming that, several generations from now, there has been no major war and extreme over-crowding is the problem of the day. Struggling desperately with the task, the United Nations have finally come together and brought forth a "Bill of Survival Rights," backed by the power of the United Nations countries, creeds and races. Vaccination against conception, long banned in many areas, is now legal and in fact compulsory.
>
> To preserve the rights of the individual, all persons, except those obviously unfit by reason of severe hereditary, mental or physical defect, would be allowed to reproduce themselves, that is, each couple might have two children. After achieving this, most would be vaccinated. Certain males of superior qualifications, if married to equally acceptable wives, would be allowed to have large families. If their wives were unacceptable, artificial insemination from these males into suitable women, (probably with consent of their unsuitable husbands, with some sort of compensation for their wounded pride) might be done. Stored semen from great men of the past could be used in specially selected cases. An extension of this idea, which would infringe more on our cherished right of selection, would be to refuse marriage licenses to those considered unsuitable, or give them conditional licenses in which the number of children allowed, either natural or by insemination, would be part of the contract. One further advance in knowledge, the transplantation of ova from one female to another, and possibly the storage of ova, would enable us to preserve the characteristics of desirable women as well. Such transplants have already been done in animals. The effect on the ugly duck mother of producing a swan I leave to the psychiatrists and the authors of new children's fairy tales.[11]

Nothing is more audacious in McClatchie's statement than his reference to preserving "the rights of the individual."

Other scientists hold to the elimination of undesirable elements in

[11] Sam McClatchie, M.D., "The Ultimate Injection," in *Amazing Stories, Fact and Science Fiction*, vol. 35, no. 2, February, 1961, p. 83.

the population, and by this the politically and religiously undesired are meant, i.e., "the over-principled":

> A Columbia University professor recently stated that "Fifteen per cent of the over-principled population should be encapsulated." This means locked up in a mental hospital, perhaps to be rendered harmless by a free lobotomy. A lobotomy is a permanent "don't-care-pill" administered with a knife.[12]

This is in principle no different from Pharaoh's attempt to destroy all Israelite males at birth and thus eliminate the race. From that time to the present, totalitarianism has used population control extensively.

Dr. Paul R. Ehrlich of Stanford has declared that the ideal population of the United States would be 150 million, 50 million less than the 200 million at the time he made his statement.[13] On what grounds a population figure represents a desirable population is, of course, an entirely subjective judgment.

The planners themselves cannot always agree on whether there is a need for more or less people. They are agreed on the necessity for control.[14]

In practice, however, planners have both encouraged and discouraged population growth. Red China for a time sought to increase the birth rate. Later, a desperate effort began to reduce the population, which may already have been reduced by famine and purges. Various fantastic "remedies" for fertility, including the eating of tadpoles as an oral contraceptive, and the separation of couples, have been used.[15]

From the Soviet Union, conflicting reports appear, expressing both

[12] Tom Anderson, "Are You a Mental Case?" in *The Presbyterian Journal*, vol. XXI, no. 36, January 2, 1963, p. 11.

[13] "Fearless Doctor's Anti-motherhood," in Paso Robles (California) *The Daily Press*, Thursday, January 4, 1968, p. 3.

[14] See Max Ledner, "Controlled Population in the Future," Oakland *Tribune*, Friday, January 14, 1966, p. 24; John D. Rockefeller 3rd, "The Greatest Challenge of Our Time," *The Reader's Digest*, October, 1966, pp. 85-90; D. J. R. Bruckner, "Expert on Cities Sees Grave Population Peril,' in Los Angeles *Times*, Thursday, April 14, 1966; George Getze, "Man's Survival Hopes Dim, Zoologist Says," Los Angeles *Times*, Tuesday, February 22, 1966, Part II, p. 1; also in the L.A. *Times*, Sunday, March 6, 1966, Section C, p. 1, Harry Nelson, "Life or Death Crusade — Man vs Birth Rate."

[15] Henry Palm, "Tadpole Birth Control Myth," Oakland *Tribune*, Friday, January 12, 1964, p. 7; "Chinese Birth Control," in *Parade's* Intelligence Report, *Parade*, March 6, 1966, p. 23.

Soviet official concern over the growth of the population,[16] and official dismay over the declining birth rate.[17] In the Soviet Union there is both official action to promote birth control and limit population, and also to reward an increased birth rate. In connection with the effort to reward birth, an amusing episode occurred in 1965:

> A recent news report told about Russia's unwed mother who won the "Mother Heroine" award for 1965 by giving birth to her tenth child. After the award was duly presented amid great acclaim, the "Soviet Russia" newspapers exposed her as an unwed mother who, indeed had borne 10 children, each from a different man. Eight of the ten had been turned over to state homes and the two at home, whom the state was supporting, were literally starving because the woman and her present lover were spending the kids' support money on vodka.

> The Soviet press says the error happened "because no one bothered to check up on her." The newspaper says, "Blasphemy has been performed over the sacred word 'Mother.' "[18]

In East Europe also, we are told there is a declining population.[19] In Romania, the declining birth rate led officials to decree that abortions, previously promoted, be illegal, and, within a year, officials were claiming a "baby boom."[20] In Yugoslavia, however, abortions continue in state clinics, and some women have up to 40 abortions in a lifetime, with the country's total annual abortions numbering 500,000, and the births 400,000.[21]

How can we reconcile these contradictory efforts at increase and limitation, encouragement and discouragement of birth? When both occur at the same time in one country, as in the Soviet Union, what is the cause? The problem lies in *the plan*. *The scientific plan fails to bend to reality, and therefore reality is forced to conform to the*

[16] "Population Growth Worries Kremlin," in Oakland *Tribune*, Wednesday, April 6, 1966, p. 46-A.

[17] Richard Reston, "Soviet Birth Rate, Size of Families Declining," Los Angeles *Times*, Part I, p. 15, Monday, January 9, 1967.

[18] Butler D. Shaffer, "Is Our Leader Worried About Image?" in *The Register*, Santa Ana, California, Wednesday (m), February 22, 1966, p. A12.

[19] "East Europe's Worry: Birth Control Too Effective," *The Register*, Santa Ana, California, Thursday (m), July 7, 1966, p. A18.

[20] "Romania Faces Population Hike," in Paso Robles, California, *The Daily Press*, January 3, 1968, p. 4; Flore Lewis, "Romanians Resent 'More Babies' Decree," Oakland *Tribune*, Friday, November 17, 1967, p. 20 A; "Two Mothers to a Bed," San Francisco *Chronicle*, Friday, December 1, 1967, p. 11 E.

[21] Ray Moseley, "Woman, 45, Enters Clinic to Have 32nd Abortion," in Pasadena, California, *Star-News*, January 21, 1968.

plan. But the planners include men who need more slave labor (i.e., socially controlled labor) to fulfil their plans, and also men who must feed that labor. More production is needed: hence, more babies to provide labor for production. There is a lack of food and materials for consumption by the labor force, i.e., there is over-consumption in relation to the supply: hence, reduce the number of the consumers. Thus, one division of planners needs more workers; another division wants fewer mouths to feed.

Since socialism fails in its attempt to manage production and consumption with the existing population, its next step becomes the production of more producing laborers, *and* the limitation of consuming workmen by birth controls. Socialism thus veers from one solution to the other, depending on which set of planners is most in favor.

There is still a *fourth* aspect of the economics of population control which deserves attention, *state planning of vocations.* The planning economy finds itself unable to cope with supply and demand, and it seeks to meet the requirements of a functioning economy by moving people to new jobs, or in a variety of ways using direct or indirect coercion to direct labor in the planned channels. In a free economy, there is a natural flow of labor to necessary areas in terms of price or wage incentives. Men move from job to job in terms of higher pay, and the higher pay is possible because a heavy demand for goods in that area means greater profits. A movement of labor is necessary in any economy. The planned economy replaces the profit and wage incentive with force.

Thus, we are told that, by means of taxation and subsidies the President L. B. Johnson farm plan called for the "liquidation" of 2.4 million farmers:

> The No. 1 U. S. farm problem: how to "liquidate" some 2.4 million farmers.
>
> In 20 years, even with all the Government help for agriculture, there has been "liquidation" of 2.6 million farmers—that is, these farmers have left the land.
>
> But the exodus from farms, it appears, is only half completed at this point.

The White House takes the view that only 1 million efficient farmers could produce all U. S. farm needs. Today, there are 3.4 million farmers Thus, according to the White House, there are 2.4 million unneeded farmers.

President Johnson and his Budget Director, Kermit Gordon, both have spelled out the Administration's goal in dealing with farm problems.[22]

We are indeed told by experts who plan on the highest level, that the world's small farms must go:

Paris (AP)—Agricultural ministers of North America and Western Europe agreed Thursday that tiny plots must be merged into economically sound farmlands in order to improve agricultural income.

Meeting as the agricultural committee on the Organization for Economic Cooperation and Development (OECD), the ministers said these "structural adjustments" would help reduce the need for price supports and protection, and thus facilitate a general trade in farm produce.[23]

The contradictions in such planning have been well described by D. P. Van Gorder in *Ill Fares the Land* (1966). But contradictions mean nothing to the planners. In the Communist countries, the redistribution of labor is forcibly accomplished, but coercion to alter the economic scene is increasingly common everywhere.[24]

We have cited the four basic aspects of the economics of population control. Although these are all politically motivated and directed, they are clearly economic in impact and purpose.

A *fifth* aspect of population control, while also politically motivated and directed, is not economic. It is, however, basic, and it is the necessary pre-condition to the other four modes of control. This is *the destruction of Christian orthodoxy*, the attack on Biblical faith. These four methods of population control were common to antiquity. Their slow retreat began with the growth of Biblical faith, and the development of the implications of Biblical religion. Science as the new hope of man undergirds the returning controls. The elite scientific planners, as the new gods of creation, are increasingly

[22] " 'Liquidation' Ahead for 2.4 Million Farmers?" *U.S. News & World Report*, March 22, 1965, p. 59.
[23] Los Angeles *Times*, February 28, 1964, "Small Farms Must Go, World Experts Agree."
[24] See "Royal Revolution in Iran," *The Reader's Digest*, October, 1967, pp. 127-131.

entrusted with more and more religious authority over man. In the new morality, man is the prime experimental animal and is to be used, bred, and moved as the elite planners determine.[25] The growing surrender to the planners is a religious surrender: it is grounded in the popular assumption that the planners can lead man into paradise on earth. To counteract this religious surrender, a religious resistance is necessary.

[25] See R. J. Rushdoony: *The Mythology of Science.* Nutley, New Jersey: Craig Press, 1967.

IV

THE POSSIBILITIES OF DEPOPULATION

An analysis of the total fertility rates for the white population in the U. S. is of interest. The total fertility rate means the total number of births experienced by women bearing children when they have reached the menopause. In 1800, the total fertility rate was 7.04. In 1850, it was 5.42; in 1875, 4.55; in 1900, 3.56; in 1925, 2.84. A low was reached in 1936 of 2.10, a high in 1957 of 3.58, with a decline since then.[1] There has been a steady growth of population in the United States despite the decline in the total fertility rate. The population has increased because the fertility rate has still been better than merely reproducing the existing population, and because of immigration.

In Europe too, between 1650 and 1900, the population growth was marked. During that period there was

> (1) a steady decline in the percentage of world population inhabiting Africa; (2) a declining cycle in the percentage distribution of population in all Asia outside of the U.S.S.R.; (3) an increasing cycle in the percentage distribution of population in the two Americas and Oceania; (4) a continuing rise in the percentage distribution of population in Europe and the U.S.S.R.[2]

Populations in Asia and Africa declined in their percentage of the world population; sometimes they also declined numerically as well in limited areas. The significant fact is the marked growth in Europe and the Americas.

Why this startling difference between 1650 and 1900? The reasons

[1] Ansley J. Coole and Melvin Zelnik: *New Estimates of Fertility and Population in the United States*, p. 36. Princeton, New Jersey: Princeton University Press, 1963.
[2] Kuan-I Chen: *World Population Growth and Living Standards*, p. 51. New Haven, Conn.: College and University Press, 1960.

are deeply rooted in cultural tradition. *First*, "medieval" Europe saw a major cultural revolution in the shift from a religious emphasis on asceticism, monasticism, and the other-world to a Catholic humanism, with Scholasticism, Franciscans and Dominicans concerning themselves increasingly with this world. The secular clergy took over religious leadership progressively from the monks, with an increasing insistence on the church's relevance to the problems of this world. *Second*, the Renaissance introduced secular humanism and a this-worldly orientation into full-blown power and respectability. *Third*, the Protestant Reformation, while hostile to both Catholic humanism and the Renaissance, and insistent on God's sovereignty, was dedicated to a Biblical materialism, to the application of Christian faith to man's common life. *Fourth*, the Enlightenment re-enthroned humanism and the humanistic doctrine of progress into Western culture.

Thus, Catholic man, Protestant man, and Enlightenment man were now dedicated to conquering the material world with all the robust freshness of a confident faith. The result was intellectual, religious, scientific, educational, colonial, and biological fertility. Western man went forth to conquer, confident that God, progress, and history were on his side.

Since 1900, a new trend has set in. *First* of all, Christian missions have introduced into Asia and Africa a new faith and a new impetus. Medical missionaries have reduced the death rate, and missionary schools have introduced both Christianity and humanism, creating thereby a revolutionary ferment. *Second*, Western colonialism has introduced both Western science and technology, and Western concepts of inevitable and necessary progress. The result has been a vast charge of social energy into Asia and Africa, and biological fertility as a result of this new impetus, at the same time that pessimism and loss of faith began to infect Western culture.

There are those who see the only "natural checks on growth" as

[8] Harold F. Dorn, "World Population Growth," in The American Assembly, Columbia University: *The Population Dilemma*, p. 7f. Englewood Cliffs, New Jersey: Prentice-Hall, 1963.

[4] Alan Guttmacher, M.D., *The Complete Book of Birth Control*. New York: Ballantine Books, 1961.

disease and *famine*.[3] The only answer, when these natural checks are removed, is mechanical, i.e., birth control, which is seen as the remedy to an uncontrolled sky-rocketing rate of animal growth. The "promise" of birth-control is deliverance from an unrelenting biology.[4] Otherwise, as John F. Kennedy suggested, "Could this nation, this world, be headed for the fate of the lemming?"[5] The pressing world problem, we are told, is this "fact" of growing over-population.[6] The population explosion is creating world hunger.[7]

But is population growth so mechanical? We have cited the cultural facts which led to the modern growth. An interesting modern reversal of population growth in Ireland is cited by Bates:

> One of the best demonstrations of the action of the Malthusian propositions is shown by the population history of Ireland. Through the Middle Ages, the Irish population was presumably stable, like that of England and the rest of Europe: limited partly by the the nature of the crops, but also by the system of land tenure whereby even a serf, before he could marry and raise children, had to gain rights to land for crops or pasturage. The attempts of the English to conquer and exploit the country led to the breakdown of the traditional systems. Then, soon after 1600, the potato was introduced from America. Perfectly adapted to Irish climate and soil, this plant provided a completely new means of subsistence. According to one contemporary estimate, an acre planted to potatoes would support a family of five through the year, and a sod hut for living quarters could be easily built in a few days with the help of neighbors and friends. Children, instead of being a burden, helped take care of the potato patch.

> The Irish population started on a spectacular spree of reproduction to keep up with the means of subsistence provided by the miraculous potato. It is generally thought that the pre-potato population of Ireland was about two million. The first regular census of 1821 showed a population of 6,802,000; the census of 1831, 7,767,000; of 1841, 8,175,000. The poverty and miserable living conditions of the Irish peasant became notorious even at a time when poverty and misery were common enough everywhere, but the population continued to grow.

> Then, in 1845, disaster appeared in the form of the potato blight, a disease new to Europe. The crop was ruined that year and the next.

[5] John F. Kennedy, "The American Economic System and World Population," in Marian Maury, editor: *Birth Rate and Birth Right*, p. 77. New York: Macfadden Books, 1963.

[6] Sir George Handley-Knibbs: *The Shadow of the World's Future*. London: Ernest Benn, 1928.

[7] John Laffin: *The Hunger to Come*. New York: Abelard-Schuman, 1966.

A million or more persons died directly or indirectly from starvation, and the outward movement of the Irish population was speeded, continuing all through the century. The population in 1960 (Eire and Northern Ireland) was 4,259,000—about half the size reported in 1841. It is clear that in this case the Malthusian "moral restraint" is operating, since Ireland has the lowest marriage rate, and the oldest age of marriage, of any country. Somehow the disaster of the blight jolted the Irish culture in a way that led to an equilibrium between population and resources: which makes one wonder whether disaster is necessary before such an adjustment can be made.[8]

The relationship of the Irish famine to the exhaustion of soil by mono-agriculture, by single-crop farming, deserves attention, as does the effect of such farming on the soils of today. There is reason to believe too that pesticides may create a problem for farming and for food supplies by their destruction of animal and insect life, and their effect on the soil.[9]

Moreover, some countries, by their incompetence and political chaos, are almost certainly headed for disaster. Paul and William Paddock have placed Haiti, Egypt, and India in the "can't be saved" group in their study, *Famine, 1975* (1967).

The modern humanistic confidence in science has led to an undue confidence that plant diseases can be overcome quickly and easily, whereas the problem is a serious one, and the defeats very real. The inability of science to cope with the fungus which destroyed the American chestnuts must be cited. "Out of an estimated billion trees there were about 180 left in all North America in 1963," with no assurance these would not also die. Also the elms of this continent are going." And so on.[10]

Technology is over-rated today with respect to its ability to cope with man's problems, and science is assumed to provide a quick answer to all problems. This assumption itself is grounds for disaster.

[8] Marston Bates: *Expanding Population in a Shrinking World*, p. 16f. See also G. L. Carefoot and E. R. Sprott: *Famine on the Wind, Man's Battle Against Plant Disease*, pp. 70-91; Rand McNally, 1967; and Cecil Woodham-Smith: *The Great Hunger, Ireland 1845-1849*, New York: Harper & Row, 1962.

[9] See Rachel Carson: *Silent Spring*, Boston: Houghton Mifflin, 1962; J. I. Rodale and staff: *Our Poisoned Earth and Sky*, Emmaus, Penn.: Rodale Books, 1964; "Five Years After 'The Silent Spring,'" *Natural Food News*, vol. 5, no. 5, p. 1.

[10] G. L. Carefoot and E. R. Sprott: *Famine on the Wind*, p. 205.

But it is an assumption which comes readily to urban man, and the world today is dominated by urban centers which have little awareness of the earth-bound realities of life.[11] Urbanization has led to an imbalance in man's view of the world. Neo-Platonism and monasticism led to a non-Biblical contempt of this world. A new form of this contempt of the world has arisen out of *scientism* and *urbanization* The material realities are taken for granted and despised. A "hippie" girl summed up this attitude by her contemptuous response to a query as to the problem of food, and laboring for food: "Food *is!*"

Another factor is the disturbance to normal population growth by welfarism, which has produced a higher rate of growth among social parasites.[12] Welfarism plus the growing sexual immorality have had an effect. Geoffrey May's comments are to the point:

> When the difficulties of legal control are so great and the failures so obvious, why should the law have sought to maintain the doctrine of chastity? Why has the question of morality entered into a voluntary sexual connection which does not injure the two persons taking part in it or any third person, and which, moreover, can do no injury to the child which may be engendered by it? The answer is, that though no individual may suffer by voluntary non-marital sex expression, society conceives itself to be suffering. It is losing potential strength.

> The vital statistics support this conception. Parents who indulge in extra-marital sexual activity show a lesser fecundity than married parents, and their offspring are less likely to survive infancy. European averages indicated some years ago that while 100 prostitutes will give birth to 60 children, 100 married women will give birth to between 400 and 500 children. Of families in which there are actions brought for dissolution on the grounds of adultery a noticeable plurality have no children and only a very few have more than one child. More important is the disproportion in mortality rate between legitimate and illegitimate children. The ratio of still-births is much lower among the children of married parents. The deaths of infants born to married parents are fewer in proportion than the deaths of illegitimate infants. In England and Wales in 1926 for every 100 death of legitimate infants, there were over 190 deaths of illegitimate infants. Throughout Europe this disproportion is appreciable and in some countries even greater

[11] For an account of this urbanization, see Peter Hall: *The World Cities.* New York: McGraw-Hill, 1966.

[12] See Belva Detlof: *Welfare Wonderland.* Whittier, California: Constructive Action, 1968.

than in England. It is said that the childbed mortality of unmarried mothers is twice that of married mothers.

The consequence of these facts is that the persons who indulge in non-marital sex expression have been dying out and breeding themselves out. Unmarried women and divorced parents have few children proportionately who survive infancy. Parents who are living according to the social conventions instill in their children those same conventions. The children who in practice disbelieve those teachings will themselves have less chance of progeny. The conventions of sexual morality have thus maintained themselves.[13]

Welfarism is a revolutionary step against the realities of moral responsibility and its social power. Welfarism is an attempt to subsidize irresponsibility and penalize responsibility by heavy taxation. This is its practical effect even where it is not its intent. But the decline of a responsible middle class means the collapse of the social fabric and the decline of all. A parasite cannot survive the death of the host body.

What can cause a decline in population? Sauvy assures us that there are only four ways to meet over-population:

1. *Return to an increased death-rate,* either voluntarily, according to the more or less clearly expressed desire of some; or involuntarily, as a result of a shortage or of cataclysms, such as war.

2. *Emigration to other lands.* The population decreases by exits from the territory. This would be a geographical solution.

3. *Progress in production* of subsistence-means, sufficient to feed everyone and even to improve welfare. This is the so-called economic solution. The rhythm of growth remains, but without harmful results.

4. *Reduction of the birth-rate,* sufficient to slow down or stop the growth of the population. This is the so-called demographic solution.[14]

In one sense, Sauvy's claim that these are the only ways of coping with population is right: his four categories are broad enough to cover most things. But, in another sense, Sauvy's statement is wrong. *First,* it sees population as a growth upwards, and hence as a problem, i.e., a problem of over-population. But what if depopulation should be the problem? And what of Karl Brandt's statement that the U. S. is under-populated? Sauvy has set the problem so that

[13] Geoffrey May: *Social Control of Sex Expression,* pp. 271-273. New York: William Morrow, 1931.

[14] Alfred Sauvy: *Fertility and Survival,* p. 88. New York: Colliers, 1963.

44

the answer lies only in an indicated direction. More than once in history, men have assumed a problem and then provided an "inescapable" answer. Thus, the Japan of the shogunate had a small population as compared to modern Japan, but the shogunate believed it to be too much. As a result, the Japanese were subjected to the annual human "Mabiki," the thinning of the human crop by abortion and infanticide.[15] Again, Rome saw itself as over-populated as it faced a growing problem of welfarism with less and less financial resources. Tertullian wrote, in *De Anima*:

> The strongest witness to the vast population of the earth to which we are a burden and she can scarcely provide for our needs; as our demands grow greater, our complaints against nature's inadequacy are heard by all. The scourges of pestilence, famine, wars, and earthquakes have come to be regarded as a blessing to over-crowded nations, since they serve to prune away the luxuriant growth of the human race.[16]

For Tertullian, living in a sick age, man was sick, and there were too many people. But from our perspective, the world then was obviously not over-populated.

Second, Sauvy's statement assumes a mechanical or a self-conscious answer, a deliberate answer, or else a forced answer such as war. But is history to be read materialistically? Long before the Romans saw the barbarians invade Rome, Rome was depopulated by both a *declining birth rate and plague*. The sickness of Roman culture manifested itself in an inability to reproduce itself or to survive.

But, it is argued, modern medical science has given us a safeguard against plague. Is this true? The Rome which succumbed to the plague had far better medicine and sanitation than the virile and resistant young Rome. When the Black Death struck "medieval" Europe, sanitation, bathing, and medicine were advanced, and, not until late in the 19th century, were similar conditions of sanitation and bathing achieved.

As we analyze plagues, certain facts appear. *First*, plagues appear

---

[15] Carefoot and Sprott: *Famine on the Wind*, p. 17.

[16] Garrett Hardin, editor: *Population, Evolution, Birth Control*, p. 22. San Francisco: W. H. Freeman, n.d.

at the end of an era, at the end of an age. Plagues are thus a phenomenon of the collapse of a culture or a civilization. Boccaccio's *Decameron* is an epitaph on an era, written in 1348 in a time of flight from plague in Florence. Boccaccio's description of the plague is vivid:

> In this sore affliction and misery of our city, the reverenced authority of the laws, both human and divine, was all in a manner dissolved and fallen into decay, for (lack of) the n inisters and executors thereof, who, like other men, were all either dead or sick or else left so destitute of followers that they were unable to exercise any office, wherefore every one had license to do whatsoever pleased him. . . .

> Indeed, leaving be that townsman avoided townsman and that well nigh no neighbour took thought unto other and that kinsfolk seldom or never visited one another and held no converse together save from afar, this tribulation had stricken such terror to the hearts of all, men and women alike, that brother forsook brother, uncle nephew and sister brother and oftentimes wife husband; nay (what is yet more extraordinary and well nigh incredible) father and mothers refused to tend their very children, as they had not been theirs. . . .

> Many breathed their last in the open street, whilst other many, for all they died in the houses, made it known to the neighbours that they were dead rather by the stench of their rotting bodies than otherwise; and of these and others who died all about the whole city was full[17]

But before this radical collapse brought on by the plague, there was already an inner collapse of the old order. Significantly, those most involved socially in the world of the day died most frequently, i.e., those between 20 and 60, whereas the aged, and the very young, suffered much less.[18] In other words, the element in the population which, in terms of physical health, should have had the greatest resistance to infection had the least. But this same group was the most involved in the religious decline and moral decay of the day, and hence most vulnerable. The aged and the young were either not yet involved in the spirit of the age or were closer to an earlier certainty.

[17] Giovanni Boccaccio: *The Decameron*, Day the First, introduction.
[18] Gary K. North, "Economic Consequences of the Black Death," p. 8, unpublished ms. See also Josiah Cox Russell: *British Medieval Population*, p. 218. Albuquerque, New Mexico: New Mexico University Press, 1948.

Again, an analysis of the decline of the Indian population in Central Mexico is of interest. Lewis Hanke states:

> Another example from recent historical studies may be seen in the population estimates of Borah and Cook. They calculate that some 25 million Indians lived in Central Mexico when Cortez first landed, and that by 1548 this dense population had melted away to about 6 million. These figures are bound to re-open the question of whether the statistics of Las Casas were so "exaggerated" after all—for he had stated in 1542 that 'four million had died in Mexico since the conquest began. The lethal forces responsible for this estimated loss of 19 million human beings may have been malaria or intestinal viruses, rather than Spanish cruelty; but opponents of Las Casas who condemn him on the ground that the New World had a much smaller population than he claimed will now have to re-examine this argument.[19]

It is easy to blame everything on the Spanish, and there is no denying their greed and guilt. But there is also the reality of the psychlogical and physical collapse of the Aztecs, as well as their military failure. Was their culture not ready for collapse? Granted, they may have lacked immunity to new contagions, but the same was true of the Spaniards. Why were the Spaniards not decimated by the diseases of the Aztecs? Why were the Spaniards more resistant?

The mind and faith of man clearly affects his body. Psychosomatic medicine has demonstrated much with respect to the individual. It is time to recognize the effect of mind and faith on the social group.

The first settlers from England faced major problems in North America. Those whose hearts turned homeward most, died first of all, a significant fact.

Consider also the evidence presented by Dr. Simeons:

> Psychosomatic ailments account for the bulk of urban man's ill-health and are the most frequent causes of his death.
>
> Once the principle that the psyche can cause serious bodily disorders had been clearly stated, it soon became necessary to include an ever-

---

[19] Lewis Hanke, "The Bones of Cuauhtemoc," in *Encounter*, vol. XXV, no. 3, September 1965, p. 83. The reference is to Woodrow Borah and Sherburne Cook: *The Aboriginal Population of Central Mexico on the Eve of the Spanish Conquest* (University of California Press, 1963); see also Borah and Cook: *The Population of Central Mexico in 1548* (University of California Press, 1960). See also Charles Gibson: *The Aztecs Under Spanish Rule* (Stanford University Press, 1964).

widening variety of diseases in this category. Today it is easier and certainly safer to say which diseases are *not* psychosomatic than to enumerate those which are: their number is growing too rapidly.

. . . Psychic factors may play a considerable role in permitting micro-organisms to establish themselves in the human body and cause disease.

An example of this is asiatic cholera. Working in the midst of an epidemic outbreak of cholera one cannot help noticing the strange fact that the healthy adolescent, the busy mother and the wage-earning father are more often stricken than the very young children and the old and decripit. Cholera is caused by swallowing a microbe called a vibrio and it is known that the cholera vibrio is highly sensitive to acids. The acid that is always present in the normal human stomach is sufficiently strong to kill the cholera vibrio almost instantly. How then does the vibrio overcome this acid barrier which separates it from the small intestines where, in the alkaline contents, it can thrive and start its murderous activity?

The answer seems to be that it cannot. Only if the normal flow of acid in the stomach is shut off is the vibrio able to reach its destination. Now the one big thing that stops the flow of acid in the stomach is fear and panic. So it may come about that those most terrified of death are just the ones the cholera kills, while those too young to understand the danger and those to whom life seems hardly worth living and who fatalistically tend the sick and dying around them, may survive unscathed, because the secretions of their gastric juice is not emotionally inhibited. Fear might thus play an important role in the selection of victims and in this sense it would not be incorrect to say that even in cholera psychosomatic mechanisms can be of importance. Similar factors may be involved in the sudden onset of some cases of bacillary dysentery or in typhoid fever but not in plague, where the bacillus is injected straight into the blood by the bite of a rat-flea.[20]

Note the fact that, as with the plague, cholera affects the healthy most of all, and the young and aged least. Contrary to Simeons there are scholars who trace the incidence of plague to a change in the nature of man, i.e., a change in man's conception of his nature, a change of faith.

Dr. J. H. van den Berg of the University of Leyden in a work on *The Human Body,* as yet not translated into English, develops this thesis. Dr. van den Berg correlates each incidence of plague with

[20] A. T. W. Simeons, M.D.: *Man's Presumptuous Brain*, p. 1f. New York: E. P. Dutton, 1962

a radical development in human thought which shatters man's previous conception of himself and the world; his choice of emphasis concerning the crisis of faith can be argued. His conclusions are more difficult to challenge.

When a plague disappears, according to van den Berg, various reasons are cited. *First*, it can be held that man has now an immunity to the bacillus. But such immunity does not exist. *Second*, it can be argued that better hygiene has eliminated the plague or plagues. But there is no evidence of any correlation between hygiene and the retreat of the plague. Thus, while it can be said that, after 1840, the plague retreated from Turkey and Egypt, where better hygiene came into existence, the fact remains that it retreated also from Persia after 1840, without any change in sanitary conditions.

Third, it is sometimes held that the plague has lost its virulence, but again the evidence is to the contrary. Local epidemics after 1680 were equally severe as the preceding ones.

Fourth, it is held that the black rat, which lives closer to people, and thus communicates its fleas more readily to people, was pushed aside by the brown rat, which lives in sewers and not as closely to people, thus removing much danger of contagion. But the plague disappeared from London after 1666, and the brown rat did not triumph over the black rat until 1725.

Fifth, the Great Fire in London is credited with destroying the area of infection, but the parishes of London most severely stricken by the plague were not burned, so that cleansing by fire is not a valid argument.

Thus, van den Berg states, there has been no acceptable explanation until now for the disappearance of the plague from Europe. From 1348 to 1680, the plague was epidemic in Europe. Before 1348 and after 1680, the plague was local and brief-lived in Europe. Why the relative immunity before 1348 and after 1680?

According to van den Berg, there will never be found a reasonable explanation without resort to causes of a "metabletic" nature as well as to natural causes. A change in man's conception of himself, of his inner world, produces new relationship to the world, and a loss of older certainties and immunities. *Plagues are thus not matters of rats or rat-fleas*, but a human matter. The plague occurs, not because of rats or fleas, not because of man's environment, but because *man changes*, and therefore the world changes for him. The changing outlook of man thus is important to a history of man's susceptibility to plague.[21]

The pertinent question now is this: are we at the end of an intellectual era, and thus ripe for plague?

We are clearly in the last stages of humanism and its decay, in the last days of Enlightenment culture. As clearly as in the last days of Rome, or in 1348, we are at the end of an age. The radical disillusionment with humanism by the humanists themselves is already apparent. Sigmund Freud, a humanist, himself contributed greatly to the collapse of humanistic faith.[22]

Cultural drop-outs are again, as in the past, a telling index to collapse. The beatniks, the hippies, the student revolts, and the Negro revolutionaries are all cultural drop-outs. They hate and seek to destroy their humanistic sponsors and creators because they regard the world of humanism as a fraud. They themselves are humanists, but humanists in decay, drop-outs whose only faith is in destruction.

The world is ripe for plague. The prospects for depopulation are fearfully real; the prospects for over-population are largely fictional.

Those most involved will perish first. Those who are most involved include both those who love and those who hate this humanistic culture and have nothing else. The sterility of hate, the futility of destruction, will involve the drop-outs in self-destruction.

And those who, like Lot's wife, love the perishing world and turn back to it because they cannot live without it, they too shall perish.

[21] This writer is indebted to Miss Annette Holbhof of Gronigen, Holland, for a summary of van den Berg's thesis. J. H. van den Berg is familiar to English readers for his brilliant work, *The Changing Nature of Man, Introduction to Historical Psychology* (New York: Dell, 1964), which is relevant to the above thesis as a study of "metabletics."

[22] See R. J. Rushdoony: *Freud.* Philadelphia: Presbyterian and Reformed Publishing Company, 1965.

The drop-outs and the drop-ins have no future. Martin Luther moved freely and boldly among the plague-stricken: he was too concerned with shaping the future under God to succumb. His favorite psalm expressed his faith: "I shall not die, but live, and declare the works of the LORD" (Ps. 118:17). The future belongs to Christian reconstruction.

Appendix I

BIBLICAL REFERENCES
TO FERTILITY AND POPULATION

The Bible has numerous references to the matter of man's fertility, and it is important and necessary to understand these statements.

First of all, there are references to blessed fertility, fertility which is either a blessing from God, or is obedience to Him. Some of these passages are:

> And God blessed Noah and his sons, and said unto them, be fruitful, and multiply, and replenish the earth (Gen. 9:1).

> And you, be ye fruitful, and multiply: bring forth abundantly in the earth, and multiply therein (Gen. 9:7).

> For I will have respect unto you (if ye walk in my statutes, v. 3), and make you fruitful, and multiply you, and establish my covenant with you (Lev. 26:9).

> Thy wife shall be as a fruitful vine by the side of thine house: thy children like olive plants round about thy table. Behold, that thus shall the man be blessed that feareth the LORD (Psalm 128:3,4).

> And all these blessings shall come on thee, and overtake thee, if thou shalt hearken unto the voice of the LORD thy God. Blessed shalt thou be in the city, and blessed shalt thou be in the field. Blessed shall be the fruit of thy body, and the fruit of thy ground, and the fruit of thy cattle, the increase of thy kine, and the flocks of thy sheep. Blessed shall be thy basket and thy store. Blessed shalt thou be when thou comest in, and blessed shalt thou be when thou goest out (Deut. 28:2-6).

Such passages are common knowledge and are frequently cited in the literature on population and birth control.

Less familiar are the important passages which speak of unblessed

52

fertility, of population increases which only incur the wrath and curse of God. Some of these passages are:

> Therefore thus saith the Lord God: Because ye multiplied more than the nations that are round about you, and have not walked in my statutes, neither have ye kept my judgments, neither have done according to the judgments of the nations that are round about you: Therefore thus saith the Lord God: Behold, I, even I am against thee, and will execute judgments in the midst of thee in the sight of the nations (Ezekiel 5:7-8).

> For thy waste and thy desolate places, and the land of thy destruction, shall even now be too narrow by reason of the inhabitants, and they that swallowed thee up shall be far away. The children which thou shalt have, after thou hast lost the other, shall say again in thine ears, the place is too strait for me; give place to me that I may dwell (Isaiah 49:19-20).

> She that has born seven languisheth: She hath given up the ghost; her sun is gone down while it was yet day; she hath been ashamed and confounded, and the residue of them will I deliver to the sword before their enemies, saith the Lord (Jeremiah 15:9).

> Thus saith the Lord, for three transgressions of the children of Ammon, and for four, will I not turn away the punishment thereof; because they have ripped up the women with child of Gilead, that they might enlarge their border (Amos 1:13).

> The Lord did not set his love upon you, nor choose you, because you were more in number than any other people; for ye were the fewest of all people (Deut. 7:7).

> Thou has multiplied the nation, and not increased the joy (Isaiah 9:3).

> If his children be multiplied, it is for the sword, and his offspring shall not be satisfied with bread (Job 27:13f.).

> But it shall come to pass, if thou wilt not hearken unto the voice of the LORD thy God, to observe to do all his commandments and his statutes which I command thee this day: that all these curses shall come upon thee, and overtake thee: Cursed shalt thou be in the city, and cursed shalt thou be in the field. Cursed shall be thy basket and thy store. Cursed shall be the fruit of thy body, and the fruit of thy land, the increase of thy kine, and the flocks of thy sheep. Cursed shall thou be when thou comest in, and cursed shalt thou be when thou goest out (Deut. 28:18-19).

Moreover, one of the basic promises of the Bible is the declaration that God is Creator of all things by His sovereign act: Genesis 1:1; Exodus 20:11; 31:17; Hebrews 11:3, etc. Because God is the Creator, He is, therefore, the absolute law-giver, and the earth is the Lord's, Who ordains the laws thereof: Exodus 9:29; 19:5; Deut. 10:14; Ps. 24:1; 50:11; Job 41:11; I Cor. 10:26,28, etc.

Because the earth is the Lord's and is to be enjoyed only subject to His laws, failure to use the land in terms of God's law, and failure to allow the land her rest, brought on God's judgment in the form of captivity. The land was allowed to remain desolate 70 years, to fulfil the sabbath rests denied her (Jer. 25:9; II Chron. 36:21). Where the land is abused, God as the Landlord casts out the incompetent tenants or brings judgment against them, to avenge the land and to enforce restitution.

Thus, the Bible speaks of a blessed fertility and a cursed fertility. The Bible declares God's ownership of the earth, and the inescapable fact of His pledge to require judgment and restitution of all who lay waste the earth. God continues always to regard the earth as His possession, but not so the ungodly. They only incur His increasing enmity as they despise and abuse God's earth.

Appendix II

THE CULTURAL DROP-OUTS

The rejection of culture, of the past, of moral law, and of the family in favor of moral and social anarchism is one aspect of the cultural drop-out in every age.

Prior to the fall of Rome, the prevalence of such drop-outs was widespread, and is well known. But in the declining years of Catholic Europe, prior to the Reformation, the drop-out movement was widespread. Wandering folk-singers and professional university students who never attended classes systematically and zealously propagated ideas of "free love." Nudist groups staged public marches to proclaim their return to the innocence of man as against the "hypocrisy" of the law-abiding citizenry. In a variety of movements, the cultural drop-outs demonstrated their suicidal impulses.

The re-appearance of such movements in these declining and last days of humanism, of the Enlightenment era, is well known. One newspaper story on the "hippies" is telling:

At Big Sur. Hippies Snub Plea to Curb Lovemaking

Big Sur (UPI)—The flower children who live in caves, culverts and shacks around Big Sur have rejected a request to stop making love for two weeks so doctors can treat their venereal disease.

"It's almost impossible to keep them apart," complained Dr. Robert Fries, assistant Monterey County Health director. "The sexual activity here is unbelievable."

Fries said Thursday the Health Department has asked the colony of hippies in the oceanside resort to put a two-week moratorium on sexual activity to keep the disease from spreading further.

"But they laughed at us," he said. "Then we suggested a three or four-

55

day moratorium. That wasn't received warmly either. Some of the hippies don't realize this is a serious thing until after they have been treated several times.

"We've told them frankly that they are developing strains of bacteria we don't know how to cope with," Fries said. "But they don't want anyone interfering with their way of life."[1]

That such activity is suicidal scarcely requires mention. But these "hippies" are not the only drop-outs. Most of Western civilization is in the process of dropping out of life; it is forsaking the last of its Christian roots to pursue its suicidal course. The implications of the humanism it has adopted are bearing fruit in an increasing and accelerating drop-out from responsibility, accountability, and life. Modern sociology and psychology, by fixing responsibility on something other than the responsible individual, by its environmentalism, is contributing powerfully to the drop-out mentality, as is education. And modern politics is simply the massive justification of the drop-out mind and of suicide.

[1] Los Angeles *Times*, Part II, p. 3, Friday, May 3, 1968.